"I Accept" - Alex

A 1st week in the ZEN life…

San Francisco
taxi

BOOK1

by

Alex SacK

www.AlexSacK.com

Alex Sack

@DigitALSack

Alex Sack/DigitALSack

ISBN: 0991189906
ISBN-13: 978-0-9911899-0-8

For the sake of why not? some events may appear out of
precise chronology.

Sack, Alex
A 1st Week In The ZEN Life... San Francisco TAXI (Book 1) /
Alex Sack

Available from Amazon.com and other retail outlets

Chapter Stills Shot by Christian Lewis
Book Design/Cover Art/'I Accept' Logo/Map by Alex Sack

For Ma

Dad taught me that a man's worth
in life is measured by what he's
done for society;
Well, people need a ride...

GOLDEN GATE BRIDGE

ALCATRAZ

THE BAY BRIDGE

Fisherman's Wharf

Marina

North Beach

Cow Hollow

Telegraph Hill

The Presidio

Russian Hill

China town

Pacific Heights

The FINANCIAL

SEA CLIFF

Nob Hill

Richmond

Western Addition

The Tenderloin

USF

Golden Gate Park

The Panhandle

Hayes Valley

sOmA

Upper Haight Lower

The Mission

Potrero Hill

Cole Valley

Castro

Sunset

Noe Valley

Twin Peaks

Bernal Heights

Bayview

Parkside

CCSF

Glen Park

Ingleside

Excelsior

Hunter's Point

SF STATE

Lake Merced

Oceanview

Outer Mission

Visitacion Valley

101

SAN FRANCISCO

SFO

Contents

Chapter 1

Cab School
(Day 1)

9am, and here I am a stone's throw from 16th & Mission - junkie central, infused with a heavy mix of Mexican illegals, hipsters and red-light runners.

My four-day class at Cab Driver Institute is here, housed up three flights in a worn-down, antiquated, former union building imbued with the soft squeal of a (hopefully) broken burglar alarm that wafts through the air. The elevator is slow to the shared office space where Rose runs her show.

An older cabbie woman, heavy set with a great sense of humor and stories galore, Rose reminds me of my mother. She owns her own "school" and, when not driving twice a week, organizes taxi drivers in an unofficial union all while keeping steeped deep in San Francisco cabbie politics.

Back in '73, Rose quickly realized that any hopes of a living she could pursue based upon her master's in Middle English would not prove nearly as lucrative as the cabbie job that had once-upon-a-time paid for her studies.

Seemingly happy despite an intermittent emphysematous hack, dues from years of driving amongst clouds of CO_2, Rose is queen of her circle.

Upon arrival with the prerequisite driver's license, pen, Thomas Guide map book, comfortable shoes and "smile", it seems I was remiss in not bringing in some necessary form stamped by the M.T.A. (Mass Transit Authority).

Rose readily admits her website needs updating to mention the requirement, but it seems her webmaster recently died.

Anyway, it immediately becomes apparent that I am not the only one in our class of five who is missing prerequisites: Samhil (former Chicago cabbie from Somalia who at one time raised camels) also didn't have his M.T.A. form, Abdul (sleeper cell member from Yemen) didn't have his Thomas Guide, and Gomer (who previously raised peacocks in Redding, CA and is quite possibly the dumbest person I have ever met) was late, forgot his Thomas Guide, M.T.A. form, *and* the $125 cash tuition. (There was also Vishnu, but somehow he had everything.)

So, off we scuttled to fix amends post-haste!

Samhil and I split a cab to the M.T.A. office - located just a few blocks away on South Van Ness. (Not sure what happened to Gomer.)

Once at the M.T.A. - after flashing ID, signing-in with security, and being screened through a metal detector - Samhil and I headed to the 7ᵗʰ floor where we proceeded to a bullet-proof glass window to procure the necessary forms... and get them stamped.

There a young, and highly impatient, Asian woman began stoically asking Samhil and me four questions designed solely to affirm we could speak and *understand* English.

Among the questions, I was asked if I possessed a commercial driver's license to which I replied "no", chuckled nervously, and asked in return if it was required.

Shit. Was class over before it even started!?

It was not; Asia simply needed to verify that I understood the question, *in English!*

Now, all within the span of a half hour, it was back to class - by way of splitting another cab with Samhil - our stamped M.T.A. forms in Hand!

Side note: I remain truly baffled how Abdul could possibly have passed his English test. Surely his sleeper cell provided him a forgery.

So, the next couple of hours at class were spent under Rose's guidance flipping through our Thomas Guide map books and getting tips on who the best tippers are, the ultimate being lawyers from New York who at one time worked in the service industry. "Have you ever seen a doctor come to YOU? All limos."

Other Rose pointers included the likes of, "When scouting a street fair for flags, drive along the street at the *top* of the hill," as drunks don't like to walk uphill.

Ah, which brings us to the "Vomit Charge" - by law, $100 *plus* the original fare.

The charge is on account of that precious time is wasted cleaning up vomit (though apparently you will have a homeless associate on-call and ready to do an immaculate job for a twenty).

And if the drunk refuses to pay? Lock the doors and drive to the nearest police station with a citizen's arrest. (Oh, the ride to the police department is chargeable, too) :)

However, it turns out a citizen's arrest need never come into play as once this is threatened, your passenger will NOT refuse the charge. Explaining a night in jail to the family, it seems, is never preferable to shelling out the hundred bucks.

So, once finished with the map studies, some safety tips and various tricks of the trade, us boys are sent off to the aforementioned nearby 16th & Mission corner with a shared clipboard in hand to study this sketchy intersection's traffic scene, in detail...

How long does it take for pedestrians to cross? Approach them and ask if they felt they had enough time to cross. Ask a disabled person, too. What street signage was observed? What traffic violations were observed? What legal and illegal activities made the intersection unsafe? Blah, blah.

Mind you, this was a difficult team to come to consensus with; even when just timing the durations of red, yellow and green lights! I ultimately gave up and just ended up watching Samhil, Vishnu and Gomer deliberate - while Abdul just stood there dumbfounded.

Very sweet guys, though. At one point I ran out for coffee, and when I'd returned I found that Samhil had bought a banana for me in my absence. He passed it on with a warm smile and a generous tip about the vendor, "Best price for produce in the city."

At about 5 o'clock, having just finished with our assignment at the corner, it was back to Rose - who only then realized we had all missed lunch (unless just feigning as a ruse to make up for lost time at the start). An apple was given to all and cordial good byes exchanged, until day two.

So it's off to home, and diving into the estimated hour and a half of homework - however unlikely to be checked. After months on the couch, I can't wait to start my new life, although I have the feeling I just have.

THIS is why my former career-in-a-cubicle fades in the rearview...

Chapter 2

Yield

My week of cab school is finished. And I'm now done with signing-up (and waiting two months!) for the first open one-day M.T.A. class/final exam – as well as clearing a multitude of various other bureaucratic obstacles.

Anyway, I passed. Yay!

The final M.T.A. class/exam was a trip. Aside from the one applicant who got expelled for cheating on his final exam - after failing his previous try two months earlier, there were others...

That M.T.A. class had the likes of Ahmet; a nicely kempt western-dressed Asscrackistani who was quite taken aback when instructed by the examiner that drivers are legally obligated to transport passengers' dogs when presented with the situation. Well, ok. There are two caveats...

You can decline if vicious (the dog, that is) or exempted via a doctor's note verifying allergy (the driver).

Aghast, Ahmet inquired if he could at least "put the dog in the trunk". ShaNayNay the Examiner, with true professional demeanor and displaying the patience of a saint, proceeded to spend the next five minutes in a volley explaining "the problem of putting the dog in the trunk" with the oft repeated return from a confused Ahmet,

"But, *Why* can't we put the dog in the trunk?"

(Seems Mitt Romney missed-out on his soul 2012 running mate.)

Anyway, the next step after receiving certification from the M.T.A. in the form of a taxi picture ID called an "A Card", was my orientation at a *real live* cab company! (The one I surreptitiously paid 25 bucks to for a Letter of Intent, in order to be allowed to pass go and sign-up for the final M.T.A. class/test.)

And Citizen's Cab has characters...

Jesus is the slow-drawled, Casablanca-tie wearing manager at Citizen's Cab. He's actually a very kind man, and brings the jokes. He gives out snack packs of raisins through the metal tray under the bulletproof glass to all drivers turning in their end-of-shift gate money (cab rental), waybills (trip log), and keys, etc.

At orientation, after having the applicants sign a host of legal papers no one has time to read through, Jesus sends us off in a cab on a road test with a veteran Citizen's cabbie; this being the final, *final*, test before the Holy Grail of employment.

I wasn't nervous. Though, in retrospect I should have been. I passed, "barely".

All are assigned letter grades, and I got a C minus. Apparently, I "follow too close" and drive a bit too "aggressively". Aggressively!? Isn't that *mandatory* for a cab driver?? (Ok, ok. I'm being defensive.)

Anyway, along with me in the group of three on our road tests was a 50-something year-old lesbian from D.C. that I hit it off with pretty good.

Maddow was confident, smart, and organized. She got a C. And boy was she pissed!

We made a compact afterwards to not let Jesus know anything more than just "we passed".

Also in our test group was Hamid. (Ok, I don't *really* know his name, but it was probably "Hamid".)

He was the first to be tested. And on account of his earlier frequent and awkwardly-timed interjections into my and Maddow's converse, I was not expecting much from Hamid. I think all had a deep sense of foreboding on this one...

After he soundly failed the unlock-the-door test and had to be kibitzed to resolution, we all got into the cab and headed for 101, with Hamid behind the wheel. All made sure seat belts were tightly fastened. (No one was gonna fail *that* test now!)

(Jerk! … SCREECH!! … Squeal!)

"Relax," our judge, jury and executioner urged with calm - until we reached the yield to 101 north…

It was then that Hamid began violently shaking (not the *cab*, Hamid!) before pulling to a complete stop halfway over one of the two solid whites flanking the yield lane to the highway. And there he stayed…

No competing traffic was imminent, but we just stayed there half in the yield lane, waiting.

Eventually, a pick-up truck that had been trailing us to the highway reached the limit of his exasperation and angrily sped around us at the yield and on towards the 101 north on-ramp. But forthwith, Good Buddy was pulled-over for this executive decision by C.H.P. Seems the motorcycle cop was hiding there staking-out the on-ramp.

Poor guy. Never had a chance. Totally set up.

Hamid takes San Fran!

Anyway, after eventually (and erratically) actually making it onto the highway, Hamid follows-up by completely blowing-off our examiner's direction to "take the next exit at Vermont Street".

And with this, our judge calmly instructed Hamid to get off at the next exit and pull over. It was then he gently broke it to Hamid that he was a "nice person", but failed the test (only after retrieving the cab keys, of course).

I really felt for Hamid. It's sad seeing an old Asscrackistani on the verge of tears.

But for the rest of us, it was back to Jesus to sign up for a couple of on-call shifts and fork-over our $100 (cash only) starter deposits - to be claimed by Citizen's Cab in the event of crash.

<u>Of note</u>: $5 is to be added incrementally to our daily gate (cab rental) until a full $500 deposit is reached.

Anyway, I'll cap this chapter the way Jesus began our orientation...

The Pope has a big speech at the U.N. and the Pope-mobile breaks down. He flags down a cab who is *shocked* to find that he is picking up the Pope:

The Pope says to the cabbie, "My son, please let me drive. I'm late for my big speech and I know the fastest way to the U.N."

The cabbie figures, "Who am I to argue with the Pope?" and promptly gets in back.

While en route to the U.N., a patrolman pulls over the cab for speeding. And as he approaches the Pope in the driver's seat, he jumps back in disbelief.

The patrolman calls-in to his Sarge, "Sarge, I just pulled over someone for speeding and I don't know what to do. He's REALLY important."

"Well," the Sarge says, "Who is it? The Mayor?"

"No. Bigger," says the patrolman.

"Who? The Governor??"

"No. BIGGER."

"Don't tell me you pulled over the PRESIDENT!"

"No. EVEN BIGGER!! I don't know, Sarge. But whoever he is, he's got THE POPE driving him!!!"

Yeah, I 'Accept'.

Chapter 3

Monday
My 1st Day Driving

Well, after six months at home (milking unemployment *and* my savings) and wading through a three months-long San Francisco Mass Transit Authority bureaucracy to become taxi driver legal, I am finally driving and making money, sorta.

Cab driving is fun! What was I doing behind a desk all those years??

I got to see the most stunning sunrise this morning as it was just peeking up over the bay all orange and red - my day shift started early, 3:30am. (Ok, this is a mixed blessing.)

I've already met a couple of interesting people so far that I have had the option to talk to, or not. And have seen them all off before any could become (total) boors.

I have been going where I want, when I want, and have borne witness to all sorts of amazing views in one of the most beautiful cities in all the world. And all while getting paid! (Sorta.)

Ironically, I feel like I am actually doing more social good than I was when I was back working ops in clean-tech. For instance, I've already picked up a handful of old and infirm fares today handed-off to me by family, or employees at various assisted-living facilities.

You see, Socialism... er, "San Francisco values" has it so that there's a "Paratransit" program for poor folks and invalids in need of free or low cost intra-city transit. They get vouchers for cab rides to the supermarket and doctor's visits and the like. And they USE them!

E.g., earlier today I drove a fantastically brittle elderly Chinese woman (completely foreign to the English language) to an old folks home in Chinatown, from her physical therapy joint in the Tenderloin.

Interesting fact: The Tenderloin is San Francisco's red-light district and got its name from the police of yore. Apparently, they got paid extra to work this dangerous beat and could hence afford to "bring home the tenderloin" to the family. But I digress...

At one point mid-ride, due to the stark white motionless face that consistently greeted me with each glance in the rear view, I became sure that my elderly Chinese passenger had died in back.

(Though I couldn't rightfully say with confidence that she was alive when they put her in.)

As I did not immediately recall Rose's cab school protocol for dead passengers, and my M.T.A. rule book was out of reach, I decided to just not look in the rear-view until we arrived at Lady Wu's destination.

Once we did arrive at the Chinatown Center For The Soon To Be Deceased, I pulled-up and parked as close as I could to the entrance - which translated to a spot in an adjacent alley. Then, it was out of the cab and back to help my fare out of her hears... er, taxi.

It was at this moment that I was caught, *lulled* by the most unusual ethereal wailing of Chinese quarter-tone vocalizations and Erhu (look it up) floating down from this foggy, haunting alley.

(Ok, it wasn't really foggy. But it paints a good picture, eh?)

I traced the Siren source to a gaggle of elderly Chinese playing some crazy-cool but-really-off traditional music from inside some kind of recreation room a little up the alley, drifting from an open door there.

Once Lady Wu was securely out of the taxi and up on her feet, which entailed about five minutes of creaking bones and very careful cane placement, she began to nudge me with her cane and motion towards the open door, the source of the hypnotic cacophony.

I forged on, providing support for Wu's attempt to take the hill:

Right foot two inches, breathe, pause…
Left foot two inches – GROooooAAAN, waver, breathe, and pause…
Right foot…

Well, you get the picture.
Ten minutes (and eight feet) later, we had arrived at the back door… and curb.
What the hell was a curb doing there?!?
But praise Confucius! Right then, at that moment, emerging like a spirit from the non-existent fog… Wu's Sherpa appeared! He came down from the alley, meeting us at the gate of that great recreation room on high. Yes!
Lady Wu's Sherpa approached nodding and smiling and taking control verily of Lady Wu's arm. He goes on to proceed in guiding my Lady in her epic quest to conquer Mount Ev… er, the curb. I carried her purse.

Five minutes later…

Once at the summit, I handed Wu's purse to my relay and made a beeline for the cab.

Query: How could Lady Wu possibly lift a 20lb. purse??

Anyway, all said and done it is quite a relief to be working, despite (or maybe because of) all the strange challenges - à la above.

I feel that I've finally graduated to the *real*-world insanities, up from the practice ones.

I do 'Accept'.

———

That said, starting out this morning was weird... The strangest thing for me was taking money from strangers. I've always been bad with money. And historically I've often felt awkward when exchanging cash in more personal scenarios, such as these.

So, as a crutch I've found safe haven this first day in mantra recital: "I'm a professional" and "*this* is your livelihood now" and by reminding myself that my time and effort are *worthy* of remuneration.

Still, that first exchange as a cab driver saw me sweating, not knowing how to tactfully broach that "now was the time for remittance".

"That'll be $7.55, please," those first words came, voice cracking.

The cab filled thick with silence. And I swear that fare took *forever* shuffling through her purse to secure my bounty. Then, the panic:

"What is she gonna tip me? *How* is she gonna tip me? Do I ask if she needs change? What happens if she gives me a credit card?? Jeez. How do I ask about adding a tip to a credit card without sounding presumptuous!?"

Suddenly, a comforting voice came emanating from deep within,

"There is an *understanding* between fare and driver... nay, a 'bond'. The *deal* is understood. All will know the dance. You will not charge for the occasional therapy session, but there IS a meter running. And once that door shuts at the end of the ride, warm feelings shall suspend."

Whoa.

I heed the voice, and my first day progressed a little bit easier. I found silence truly proving golden, and only even had to mention the amount of the fare two more times.

"The Bond" did indeed abide.

But, I gotta get my game on tomorrow. I only walked with 35 bucks.

Chapter 4

Tuesday
Grace

I laid awake most of last night stressed about the 35 bucks. And it looks like I'm gonna have to get used to a new circadian rhythm.

But while I was tossing, I came to the conclusion that nothing is really in my hands. OM. This means Grace is supposed to come soon, right?

Well, the relent *did* make me less stressed. Hmm. After all, nothing really sucks at this very moment. San Francisco is pretty. And I actually do like my new job, so far (question of money aside). I haven't been evicted, yet.

Anyway, it's an "on-call" situation with shifts until I prove myself. It's kinda weird. I'm actually *on* the schedule two days this week - Monday and Friday, but with *no assigned cab.*

This translates as me somehow having priority over those drivers not on the schedule, but I still have to wake up and call-in to the office to see if there's a cab available.

And I understand to get the worm, you have to call-in *early.*

2:00am:
   "X$@%^!!   X$@%^!!   X$@%^!!"

My iPhone alarm goes off.

Damn. Gotta change that alarm tone.

It's Tuesday; I'm not on the schedule today. But I call-in to Citizen's Cab to see if I can work.
   A guy named Kojak is working the office.

Kojak: "Uh, Sack… Sack. Don't have anything now. I'll call you if something comes available."

Sack: "Ok."

(ZZzzzzZZzzzz.)

6:14am:
   "X$@%^!!   X$@%^!!   X$@%^!!"

Damn, GOTTA change that.

Sack: "This is Alex…"

Kojak: "Sack, come in. I got a cab for ya."

Cool. *And* I got to sleep-in after a rough night. The sun is even up! (Mixed blessing.)

But how much past my gas and gate, if anything, will I make in the time I have left to drive today? Hmm. Whatever.

Later, at the lot...

I park my personal ride outside the Citizen's Cab lot fence, on the edge of San Francisco in the industrial Bayview district - an area full of rusty scrap yards and strewn-about oil drums, lumber yards and the like.

I forgo the window with the bullet-proof glass and head back into the office. I've heard it can be a good move for garnering favor with the office worker and dispatcher du jour. A new driver can learn a lot too, from playing fly on the wall to the old school drivers hanging out back there shooting the shit.

However, as I'm in so late today there is only one driver back there now - aside from Kojak working the office, and a dispatcher I've yet to make the acquaintance of.

Kojak goes over to a peg board full of keys and medallions in the front office/dispatch area there and throws me 712, a Crown Vic "spare" with 300K on her.

An old Russian driver hanging out laughs at this and says this is what the newbies get (until you can prove you can bring a cab back in one piece).

<u>Note</u>: Spares are old worn creaky cabs that I'm told are only used when the actual taxi associated with that "medallion" (city-issued taxi permit, as denoted numerically on a small rectangular piece of aluminum) is "in the shop". It should also be noted that Citizen's Cab has a shop on site with mechanics working regular business hours.

Anyway, Putin goes on to inform me that this means I'll be spending about $30 more on gas at the end of my shift, though I'll be charged $10 less on "gate" (cab rental) for driving a non-hybrid Crown Victoria. (Hmm. $30 -$10 =)

Kojak then gets in the spirit and starts-in with the schooling too,

"The only rules at Citizen's Cab are: bring the cab back by medallion time (4pm today), with a full tank of gas, make sure ya got yer gate money… and DON'T FORGET THE DISPATCHER!"

Ah, I've heard tell. The more a driver greases the dispatcher on duty's palm, the more "airports" that driver seems to magically win when "checking an order" (bidding over the radio for a call). And airports are money! (About 50 bucks a run.)

Oh, Kojak also adds, "And DON'T crash or kill anyone!!"

Two hours later, on the road...

I've been driving aimlessly around San Francisco in this rickety old Vic for two hours and I've only had two fares! (Both suits on short rides to the Financial district. Guess my old life in Admin isn't *that* far back in the rear view.)

And at some point, my knee hit some loose wires under the dash and a big spark and subsequent puff of black smoke went off. This took out the CB radio AND my turn signals and hazards.

Damn. I won't be able to take radio calls until the cab's brought back to the lot to get fixed by the mechanics. And this means down time. Jeez.

Things haven't really been happening for me here on day two. I think I'll move to Australia.

So, what to do?

Screw it. I'll wait to deal until a fare brings me somewhere out closer to the lot.

It's only been six months, but it seems like eons. To try and cheer up I remind myself about how I used to get sick of eating lunch at the same old places day to day that could be found within walking distance of my straight-life office jobs. And on *the bright side*, I now imagine that lunch could be anytime, anywhere in the city. Yeah, that's the ticket! (Not that I expect to stop and eat. Lunchtime would be money lost.)

9:30am:

I'm listening to National Public Radio.

It seems a DeSoto Cab driver failed the "don't crash or kill anyone" rule. N.P.R. said his cab was reported filled with smoke as he was coming-in fast down the Mariposa off-ramp from 280 (downtown) and burst completely into flames after slamming into a cement pillar under 280 where the off-ramp ends.

It sounds like Mohammed lived, but the crash killed his passengers, an older couple just coming in from the airport on vacation. Jeez.

Just then, driving up Sutter through Union Square (high end shopping district), it's a flag! With luggage! Two guys and two girls... with luggage! Outside a hotel. My first airport. Sweeeet!!

I pull over.

And Guys and Dolls all cram in, with one guy sitting up front.

Note: Rose had schooled that drivers should usually try to steer clear of having passengers sit up front if it can be avoided, for safety reasons (the driver's).

But these are youngish tourists - from Kentucky, they quickly offer - and all seem pretty cool.

So, we're off! And heading down 101 south at the tail end of rush hour. (I figure I'll see the mechanics at Citizen's about the CB radio and turn signals, etc. on the return from SFO.)

But only a mile down 101 just yards before the Cesar Chavez exit... 216's brakes go out.

Damn.

I pump them (hard) to no avail, mid-conversation about the weather in Kentucky.

Hmm.

No one seems to realize...

Well, I *am* a formidable conversationalist.

Ok, Cesar Chavez is the exit to the Citizen's Cab lot. But I have pangs to try and make it the ten miles more to the airport, sans brakes. Whaddya think?

(Okay, okay. That's what I thought you'd say.)

Yeah, sanity does kick-in pretty quick as I recall the N.P.R. DeSoto story that I just heard!
I choose life! And go for the *off-ramp*!? to Cesar Chavez.
(I think I'll not share the N.P.R. story with my passengers until later.)
So, I throw 216 into low gear, forgo the hazards (for lack of choice) and coast the fifty yards or so more down 101 towards the, ugh, off-ramp.
I start to nervously laugh and in informing of our predicament make light of the fact that we have no brakes by way of telling my passenegers that they get "one last 'unscheduled' tour of San Francisco" before heading home; the Citizen's Cab lot.

And Guys and Dolls are amazingly cool about it.

Whew!

We make it to the exit and coast down the off-ramp in low gear, with me working the emergency brake with my left foot while simultaneously holding the hand brake release with my left hand, and steering the taxi with my right. (Well, I *am* a drummer, people.)

Anyway, once down from the ramp, within a few level, city blocks, we safely crawl into the lot. OM!

As it seems I had grabbed the last available beaten mul... er, "spare" this morning, I scheme to finish the airport trip in my personal ride. (Totally legal, I'm sure.)

Hey, we're talking fifty bucks!

But before I can transfer any luggage, Kojak comes out into the lot to meet me with news that he's dug up another Crown Vic spare for me to go out in.

Great.

I slog back into the office to get the key, when suddenly a dumbfounded look comes over Kojak as he starts thinking aloud and mumbling something about how he just remembered how he promised *that* spare to another driver who's on their way in.

Great.

A wave comes over me as I suddenly see fit to count my blessings as I bark out "Thanks, Koj!" and exit stage left post-haste with the key.

Maybe that was Grace.

After dropping Guys and Dolls I take stock in a feeling that I seem to be getting my game on, and I strategize.

Hmm. Returning from SFO, what's the first populated commercial area I can hit in close proximity to a 101 (or 280) exit? Ah, the Mission.

Suddenly, "X$@%^!! X$@%^!! X$@%^!!"
Gotta change that!

I check the number. Hey, it's Christian! My old friend, fellow Citizen's cabbie and Spermula band mate. I answer...

Ppbbbbbt!!

He's calling worried that it was me he heard about on the news, burning and crashing and killing those tourists over on Mariposa. Anyway, I reassure Christian that it was not me, but that I did just *live* with no brakes!

Later...

Here I am, mid-day, meandering down Golden Gate and just approaching the seedy Tenderloin district.

I'm scanning the streets for flags while randomly exploring this magnificently diverse city, trying to gain perspective.

I'm stopped at a red at Van Ness. (A commercial thoroughfare.)

Hey. There's a McDonald's across the street with a parking lot. Wonder if they have a drive-thru? That could come in handy in light of the "lunchtime down is money lost" thing.

It strikes me; drive-thrus could be a source of change when needed, *and* a cheap meal to wolf down while driving. Wouldn't be too kind to my belly, though.

On that note, there is a Rose Commandment about getting out of the cab as much as possible and doing stretches and cardio and such. "While waiting in a hotel taxi line" was promoted as a good time to do this, to combat the cabbie's sedentary existence.

Rose had handed out a Xerox with generic sketches of cab drivers utilizing various parts of the cab as gym equipment. I've got it right here in my bag. Don't see it ever leaving the bag, however. I haven't really been able to bring myself to wait in hotel lines. The thought makes me antsy.

Anyway, the light turns and I cross Van Ness. But before I can turn into the McDonalds lot to investigate for a drive-thru, a 50-something white guy in a grey Member's Only jacket sporting sporadic tufts of grey hair (on his mostly-bald head) and clutching a bag of McDonald's is herky-jerky all waving his wooden cane at me, to flag I think.

Hmm. Looks kinda like a weirdo.

But, I pull over.

So, Member's Only jumps in back huffing and grunting as he settles-in before cracking a big, broad, smile revealing his only teeth as all situated on the left side of his upper jaw.

Then, with an imp-like twinkle M.O. goes on to mumble something totally inaudible before giggling out his semi-discernible destination as simply,

"Dah Cah-stro".

I catch all of this in the rear view, with waybill and clipboard at the ready to log.

But once off, Member's Only expounds with that I'm not just taking him to *one* destination, he's commandeering me on a *series* of chores!

"Uh, he, he… I neeed tah, he he, mak ah fuw quik stahps 'rouwn touwn. Ken u wate fer mee, runn en ah cuple pla-cez? Payy u. He, he…"

(With eyes all a-sparkle and cackling creepily.)

Hmm. Does this dude have money for this?

What would Rose do?

Well, one Rose Commandment was "NEVER let them out of the vehicle without paying," even if they'll "be right back".

And with this, I consent to Member's Only's request, but qualifying,

"Uh, sure. But I'll need you to leave enough to cover the fare before getting out each stop."

"He, he. Uh-k, uh-k. He, he. Heere sum munee."

And Member's Only puts aside his McDonald's and scampers through his jacket before promptly pulling out a crumpled-up list and a short stack of twenties.

He prostrates himself and hands me up one of the twenties. (All the while still a-cackle.)

I put the twenty on the shotgun seat under my Thomas Guide and clipboard, hit the meter and off we are! To destination #1: The Castro.

Ok, this is getting interesting...

Ok, ok. It was already interesting.

But Member's Only doesn't know *where* he's going in the Castro. He just wants me to drive around until he finds some Tibetan store he vaguely remembers there.

And this is breaking another Rose Commandment, "NEVER drive until the fare gives you an *exact* destination."

But what am I gonna do?

Whatever.

We make it to the Castro in like five minutes and actually find said Tibetan Store in surprisingly short order, up 18th Street.

And with our discovery, Member's Only lights up big and dives into shuffling hands as he blurts-out an exhilarated "He, he, he" and producing yet another big, broad, half-toothed smile. But before jumping for the door, M.O. surprisingly-consciously, eagerly asks first if I need more "mun-ee",

"Uh, the fare is only $13 so far. No need," I reply.

And he's off!

And back within three minutes, mandala-adorned shopping bag in hand.

Member's Only wedges in back again, and promptly reaches into his bag and begins to sensually stroke some kind of Nepalese sheet or shawl - all the while smiling huge, as he settles back with,

"He..he. He he. Taank u, taank u. Nouw, wee neeed goh too Haa-ight Streeet. Haa-ight Streeet. Therz eh hed shap der."

(Uh, there are head shops every other door on Haight Street. A little specificity, please.)

"Uh, which head shop did you mean?" I nudge.

"He, he. Uhh, jus draiv too Haa-ight. Kno wen cee. Gott-ah git ah strob lite, he, he."

And Member's Only goes back into textile love.

We get to Haight and Masonic, the beginning of the Haight-Ashbury district's commercial blocks, and I'm instructed to drive slow through the strip.

M.O. is perched up in back now like a hawk, scouring the ubiquitous store fronts for his particular head shop.

All of a sudden he launches excitedly into patting my headrest bouncing on the seat and howling,

"Sta-hhp! Heer!! He, he. He, he!!!"

And without prompting, Member's Only hands me up another twenty and waddles out of the cab, ducking inside Pipe Dreams.

...

Three minutes later, M.O. comes out of Pipe Dreams giggling and beaming, strobe light in hand.

The fare is up to $26.35 now, and I'm holding 40 M.O. dollars.

He checks his list and scratches his head,

"Hmmm. Neeed ah Cee-Dee. Dehrz ah muesik plac dere en Mahrkit, en dah Cah-stro."

"Know the one," I assure. There's only one on Market in the Castro, "Streetlight Records."

And Member's Only flashes me yet another bright half-toothed smile in the rear view and we're off! To the Castro. Again. Jeez.

Just where does this dude get his money from? What does he do for a living? Some kinda inheritance? Wait... This is San Francisco!

G.A.

Government Assistance!

We arrive lickety-split to Streetlight Records back in the Castro, and I preemptively offer that another twenty is not yet necessary.

And he's off!

While I wait, I ponder how relieved I am that dude has money and is forthcoming, however strange.

But, what the hell? Why is he going to all these random places at the not so insignificant expense of a cab ride? Dude doesn't seem too high on the financial ladder. And the bus system in S.F. ain't *that* bad. Whatever. I and my landlord *both* appreciate Member's Only. I shan't complain.

Anyway, three minutes pass fast and he's back, cackling in triumph and on a roll...

"He he... He he... Ken wee goh... Ken wee goh... too Disskownt Bilderz Suhppli en dah Mi-sson naow? I neeed sum boltz nd sum wahsherz fer mi dee-zin. He, he."

And Member's Only throws me up another twenty. I put it with the other two on the shotgun seat, as the meter hits $37.55.

"Mission and 13th it is," I confirm. And we "goh".

Hmm. For his "dee-zin"?

We make it to Discount Builders on the border of the Mission and SOMA in about five minutes and I wait in the lot as M.O. runs in for his bolts and washers.
Once back, Member's Only seems to have lost his usual glow and half-toothed grin. He looks... *uncomfortable.*

"Ken wee goh mi hoh-tel?" M.O. moans, adding a subdued "he, he" almost as if an afterthought. " Iss jus fuw blahks waay en Sowth Ven Nes, offah sixkteeh en Mi-sson."

"Sure."

Hmm. Wonder what's wrong?

As if reading my mind, Member's Only explains with a now seemingly forced half-toothed grin,

"Neeed too drahp off dah chak-a-late peaple," with a muted, "He he."

Ohhh, he's going back to his crack-head S.R.O. hotel to crap. Jeez. Guess the McDonald's kicked-in.

Wonder if they have private bathrooms at The Mission Hotel? Probably not.

Anyway, we get to 16ᵗʰ & South Van Ness quick and I again preempt in informing Member's Only that we're good on twenties for the moment. He lurches all pained, out of the cab.

Hmm. Maybe a change of pants is in order too? I check the back for damage. Then wait with doors locked, as I observe all the junkies, dregs, pimps and thieves drag, swagger and slither-by mixing-in amongst the hipsters, techies and hard working Mexicans that define the Mission.

Ten minutes later...

Member's Only is back. And so is his grin and bright jovial disposition,

"Ahhhhh, he he. Dah chak-a-late peaple r hah-pppy nah-ow. He he, he he. Ken wee goh, ken weee goh, too Tahp Plastikz nahow?"

Hmm. I don't know it.

"Tap Plastics?" I fish.

"En Sowth Vahn Nes. Jus ah fuw blahks awaee. Sho u. He he."

En route, I finally break; I MUST know!

"Uh, I know it's none of my business. But do you mind if I ask what you're working on?"

And with this, Member's Only swells and beams and grins like he has not thus far, big as the moon, eyes full a-twinkle flooding with love and elation, and wholly unable to contain his giddiness.
Hands all a-shuffle, M.O spills the beans with a mad genius fervor,

"Ey, he he, puhting too-getherr, he he, frum planz ey bin werkin' fer sickz munths, he he, he he, ferr, he he, wehl, ey kall et... 'The Sex Machine 2000'. Nd wen ey dun, he he, he he, etz gunna git mee ah GURL-FEN! Yuhp. He he. I aredi haav dah hammuck nd sum udda pahrtz. Buh wen Tahp Plahsticz cutz mee sum flerecent ore-ang plexi-glaz, ahl dah pahrtz wil bee, he he, redy tah asehmbl, he he. Nd DEN, ey gunna git mee ah GURL!!"

"O-kay..."

We get to Tap Plastics *fast*, and Member's Only throws up another twenty and gets out, list in hand and mumbling, all the while wholly focused on some kind of dimensions he has written on his list.

He barely turns to say,

"Bee rii-iit baak."

The fare's at $63.45 now. We've been driving around for close to two hours (with the meter mostly running at the slower idling rate) and my cab is due back at the lot and gassed-up at 4. And that's soon.

I may have to call this before I can take M.O. back home, or wherever else he may be going. Hmm.

How do I broach this?

Honestly, I guess.

I *can't* be late back with the cab. That'd be a $15 late charge (for the first one to fifteen minutes late) and a pissed-off night driver. But, we'll see how long this takes.

Three minutes later...

Member's Only comes out.
Well, ok. Whew!
But... he's empty-handed. Hmm.
He leans-in the shotgun window with,

"Dey gunna kut mee mi plaahstic. Et bee dun 'rauwnd fiht-eeen minitts."

Damn.

I don't think I can wait. Hmm.

I break the news.

"Uh, I have to get the cab back now. I'm real sorry, but we're gonna have to settle the fare. I can't be late back with the cab or I'll be charged $15 by the night driver. But, hey! Here's a card for Citizen's Cab. Call them! Someone'll come get you when you're ready. They're good people."

But, Member's Only is overcome with a look of sadness and confusion, and dejection... like an abandoned pet.

Wha?

I think he'll *miss* me!

As the concept settles though, you can see in his face as Member's Only starts to accept.
And with that, he reaches into his jacket to retrieve and throw me yet another *two* twenties!

I wave him off, objecting,

"It's ok! The fare's only at $73.65 now and you've already given me $80 so far. *Two* more twenties is way too much!

But Member's Only goes into his head to calculate, and then goes on to insist I take it,

"Neeed tah th-ip u goood. Ta-ankz."

And with this we part. With me a $120 richer thanks to the San Francisco tax payer, Member's Only and the Sex Machine 2000!

It's my second day cab driving, and I'm walking with 135 bucks.

I 'Accept'.

Chapter 5

Wednesday
Ron Jeremy & Anna Nicole

I'm pretty conscious about how new I am to this game. And I'm very much on edge. But it's a good "very much on edge". It's been a rush. And yup, six months of sitting at home unemployed was *definitely* enough.

My first week driving has thus far been trial by fire, just getting comfortable with the dance. But even more so, getting to know the roads!

I keep Rose's Commandments churning in my head. But getting to know the city was not so much a Rose *Commandment* per se, it was the subject of 90% of cab school!

Anyway, in practice I'm still at the very beginning of work in progress. And I suspect this will be so for months to come.

One big revelation I've gleaned already in my first two days of driving though, is that people (myself included) generally know how to get from point A to point B when driving *personally*, but we don't usually know the NAMES OF THE STREETS we use to get there.

But I'm a professional now. (Visualize a straight back and chin held high.)

When a passenger jumps in my cab and requests, "1 Maiden Lane," the correct response is *not*, "Duh, Wha??"

But, wha??

Do I shuffle clumsily through my Thomas Guide map book? Or break out my iPhone? Nope.

Already in my two weeks, I have evolved…

"And do you have a preferred route?"

Genius!

This is my newly discovered lifeline. And I've grabbed onto it and held for dear life.

Yup, genius. This technique ambiguously shields me from looking green, *and* it schools me. I figure people generally know their regular ride, and I can learn from them. I've so far sensed most passengers generally appreciate the control, anyway.

What's that? When they decline to offer a route? Well, then they don't realize that I'm screwing up their ride! It's a win-win.

So, in addition to getting to know the roads and navigating various social conventions with Citizen's, competing cabbies, bikes, pedestrians, passengers and such, there is the *logistics* of becoming one with all the tech.

I knew I was starting out on a new career. I just didn't realize it would be at helm of the Borg mothercube!

There are smart phones and Verifones and meters and radios and cords coming outta every orafi... er, all fighting for the cab's "dash-board real estate" as the kids say.

Welcome to my new life in "the real space". Now I know why they call it "disruption".

5:00am:

So, I've been trying to take things a little slow my first week and get used to it all. But today is turning out to be a crazy morning from the get-go.

I'm back in the Citizen's Cab office and Kojak is sending me right out of the gate with an order up in Bernal Heights, on nearby Cortland Ave.

It's a hectic deal. I'm running out to my cab and it looks like I'll be forgoing the "sanitize" and "set-up the cab office" ritual that I've been developing over the last couple of days.

However, once out at 722 - a Prius (Yay!) - and before I can get a chance to start her, my stomach starts to rumble something awful, all volcano-like.

It seems it's not only my circadian rhythm I gotta worry about!

I have been making it a point to hit Starbucks first thing each shift: for napkins, a "tall" coffee, and the bathroom. (Bathroom access you may imagine can prove a real cab driver issue, one I have already learned firsthand.) But *this* morning, Starbucks be damned!

I throw back open the cab door and sprint across the Citizen's lot bolting for the bathroom adjacent the office, as simultaneously yelling for Kojak to wait, or re-assign, my order.

I faintly hear a dumbfounded "Gasp!" and "Why!?" the bathroom door slams shut and I just make it to the pot.

Five minutes later…

Relieved, I emerge from the bathroom and peek into the office to apologize to Kojak and see if he stills needs me for the Cortland. Kojak just laughs and says the order's gone.

Then, continuing to glow, he asks if I'm "alright".

I smile and simply answer "no" then duck back out to 722, my Prius.

Good. Now I can take my time working-in my third day on the job. Think I'll put the Cabulous phone they got installed in the taxi "On Duty" *after* Starbucks.

<u>Note</u>: Cabulous is a smartphone app that allows me to 'Accept' "mobile" orders coming from Jill or Joe Schmo looking for a taxi on the street - or from wherever, *and* orders from Citizen's Cab proper, when sent from "dispatch" - as denoted on the phone's screen. Also, Jill and Joe can track me via GPS on a real-time map on their phone when hailing by way of a "mobile" order. (Also, they have a credit card on file with Cabulous that pays automatically, with their default tip set.)

5:30am, post-Starbucks:

I'm caffeinated now, and I've made it all the way through Potrero Hill, the Mission *and* Castro and have arrived almost to the end of the Upper Haight (a.k.a. Haight-Ashbury) strip, with nothing.

Jeez.

Suddenly, Kojak comes over the radio,

"722. I got 10-64 in an accident needs back-up over at 16ᵗʰ & Clement. You have an accident kit in your cab? Can you go and assist?"

Uh. Wha? Jesus did train us on this in orientation. It means documenting the accident and taking pictures; making sure all driver's license and insurance info is exchanged, etc. Citizen's likes to have a back-up on scene to cross and dot all the flustered accident driver's Ts and Is. It shouldn't be a big deal, but I can't imagine it's money, either.

Anyway, why send the new guy? Maybe I'm just the closest driver? Hmm. Whatever.

I come back over the radio,

"722. Sure. 16th & Clement to help 10-64 with an accident. Copy."

That was fun! I'm really getting into this CB lingo. I'm told though, however tempting it is, it's *bad* form to radio-in something like "10-4, good buddy" or some such. Apparently that's trucker CB-speak, not cabbie. I already heard Tupac (some ex-gangster dispatcher) ream Maddow for trying it on Tuesday.

So, it's still dark out and I'm just approaching the end of the Haight-Ashbury strip, fareless. Why not help out with 1064's accident report? It's as good a time as any to learn.

But wouldn't ya know it? Just as I put down the CB handset, I spot a young black male in a hoodie in the street up ahead flagging me, at Haight & Shrader.

Damn!

Not only did I just lose a precious fare on this, but the Zimmerman jury just returned a "not guilty" verdict in the Treyvon thing a couple days ago, shit's heated, and I can tell by the fact that this dude's in the middle of the street, he's likely had a hard time getting one of the MANY open cabs also cruising the Haight to stop for him.

And now I can't either. This looks bad.

My top-light is on (indicating I'm available) and I've obviously been looking for flags. And now I've made it all the way to the end of the strip plainly sans-fare.

Argh!

What to do?

In the last two days when someone's tried to flag me when I'm already full (or en route to an order) I've just waved them off and attempted to sign apologetic, before keeping on.

But in light of the Treyvon injustice (and white guilt) I feel compelled to at least stop for this guy, to at least roll down the window and explain.

I stop.

And I lean over toward the half rolled-down shotgun window with,

"Dude, I'm sorry. I just got sent to help out another driver in an accident. I can't pick you up."

But Treyvon just cuts me off with a huge sigh, shaking his head incredulous with,

"Man, why u gotta *do* me like that!?"

FUCK!

I shake *my* head, gasp back big and exasperated and cut Treyvon off with,

"WHY WOULD I PULL OVER JUST TO LIE YOU!?!?"

Then I gun it outta there…

And as I'm zooming off, I just then notice three other black hoodied friends of Treyvon's semi-hidden, waiting caddy-corner for him to bag a cab. Hmm.

Either we've got a desperate racial version of the "hot chick hitchhiker whose boyfriend pops out of hiding once hottie's secured a ride" or I was gonna get jumped and robbed, maybe even in retaliation for the Zimmerman verdict.

As I said, tensions *are* high.

Maybe this accident thing just saved my life. Or maybe it just cost me a fare. I dunno. Ugh.

Anyway, I make it out to the Inner Richmond, 16th & Clement, fast… and find nothing. WTF?

I radio-in to Kojak to ask what's up.

And Kojak radios 1064,

"10-64! What's happening out there? Are you done with the accident!?"

No answer.

"I don't know what's going on, 722. I get no answer. Go ahead and leave."

Jeez.

"722. Copy. Rolling."

Then, at 15th & Clement, I come across an old Asian guy and a 20-something Asian guy standing outside a blue minivan stopped in the middle of the street near the intersection, with 1064 (a Ford Fusion) in the street too, with its front-end half hanging on the ground.

I pull over.

I get out and first approach the younger Chin to ask if I can take pictures on my phone of his driver's license and insurance info. Dude seems mellow enough, but defers pointing over at Chin Sr., indicting Sr. as the driver.

I look over to see the older Chin all amped up and running around his minivan like a chicken with... well, you know.

I ask the Citizen's Cab driver if he's exchanged info. He's a seemingly nice enough African driver I noticed at the lot on Monday.

Africa says the cops are on the way, but that he has exchanged no information yet.

I go and get the insurance card out of 1064's glove compartment, per training, and put it on the trunk of the cab where Chin Jr. is now following my lead and taking pictures of Africa's just now-produced license.

I then head over to Chin Sr. to ask for his info. But Chin Sr. just ignores the request and starts going on freaking about how the accident wasn't his fault.

Jeeeez.

I calmly assure Chin Sr. that I am not here to assign blame, just document. And can I please take pictures of his driver's license and insurance card.

Chin Jr. apologizes for Sr. not "getting" the situation as Chin Sr. just goes on steadfast ignoring my request. But Sr. now begins to run around as he also begins following my lead in taking pictures of both vehicles *and* Africa's info! (Even though Chin Jr. just did.)

I calmly persist,

"Sir, if I can just take pictures of your license and insurance info, I can move on to work. The insurance companies will figure this all out. *No one* is admitting fault right now."

Oops.

Chin Sr. flips,

"Whaa abow *miiii* wuuuk? Ayy naa wuurk DOOO!!"

Ugh.

Chin Sr. goes on to fuck with me some more as I follow him in circles around his barely-dented minivan before eventually he calms (a bit) and *finally* hands me his license and insurance.

I quickly take pictures. Then I let Africa know I'll radio-in to Kojak for a tow, and jump to get the hell outta there!

But as I turn, Africa calmly appraises his cab before he casually comes back with,

"It is fine. I will drive the cab back to the lot."

!?!?

I stop, and look curiously at the cab's front-end hanging half on the ground. And in keeping with Africa's zone, I thoughtfully scratch my beard with,

"Uhh. I think you need a tow. Maybe it's best to wait. I'll tell Kojak."

And with this, I'm off! Hitting several buttons and radioing-in to Kojak for a tow before putting myself back "On Duty".

Resistance is futile.

So, I head back toward the Haight. It's my most proximate hope for scoring an early morning flag.

Hey. Might as well see if Treyvon still needs a ride. But, hmm.

If Treyvon & Co. haven't gotten a ride by now, if they weren't gonna jump me before, they almost certainly will now!

I drive.

And...

Trayvon is indeed gone.
(Wonder how that went down.)

8:55am:

I've completed several Financial shuttles now. But I've been fixating on the probable opportunity cost of my time spent doing early morning accident duty. Been fighting with letting it go. OooOMmm.

Anyway, I'm cruising for flags in the Castro. (That sounds bad, huh.) Nothing.

In the commercial dead space between the Castro and Haight, I start to email the accident pictures from my phone (not while driving, of course) to the Citizens Cab admin woman; the one that sol... der, gave me the Letter of Intent.

She'll no doubt be calling me into the lot for the pictures if I don't preempt. And I need to be out working!

...

Ok. I've just finished emailing and right on cue, Kojak comes over the radio,

"722. I need you to come in with those pictures from 10-64."

"Uh, 722. I just emailed them to admin. There's nothing more you should need from me."

"722. The police never came and I got the driver here filling out a report. Can you bring it in? I don't have access to that email."

"722. Do you have another email address I can send to? I really need to make some money out here…"

"722. No, I don't. But, uhhh. Ok. Can you take this order in the Castro there?"

"Cha-ching! - 17 Terra Vista. Dispatch." The Cabulous phone in the cab comes chiming to life! With a dispatch! An actual dispatch! Yes! And I 'Accept'.

Then, "722. Never mind. I really need you to bring it in, please."

And the Cabulous screen goes all red with "Order Cancelled".

I put Cabulous "Off Duty" and start back to Citizen's Cab, now having lost *two* fares for an accident that I had nothing to do with.

15 minutes later, back in the office…

I'm only on my third day, but I've already developed an affinity for Kojak. And I think he likes me. But I do HAVE to vent about this huge and continued waste of my time; put differently, *money*.

(As cab drivers we are subcontracted. And as I have noticed, we seem to have some latitude to bitch.)

Kojak understands and I can tell he feels bad as I go to hand Africa my phone - so he can copy the accident info from my pix into his report.

Kojak tries to mollify me with an offer of some birthday cake sitting on the desk by dispatch, but I decline (the belly).

Right at that moment the phone rings. And Kojak heads over to sit at the dispatch station proper, and answers,

"Citizen's Cab... Uh, huh... 1400 Mission... Kink.com... SFO... Ok..."

Kojak is staring at me through the whole of the call.

Score!

"Sack, this order's due over at Kink in ten minutes. You know the S.F. Armory over in the Mission there? Go!"

"Thanks, Kojak!" And I run for my cab.

I make it over to Kink.com fast and there's some young blonde buff dude in a tight T-shirt sitting out front smoking a cigarette on the steps of the Armory.

Damn, *male* talent.

Whatever. So long as the Kink voucher's green.

<u>Note</u>: Kink.com has Citizen's Cab vouchers that are redeemable for cash at shift's end.

So, Ron puts out his cigarette at the curb and exhales a cloud half in the cab as he gets in back, sans-luggage, reeking of smoke. He dives right-in to chomping on what looks like a spinach salad,

"SFO, please. Delta," he directs between chomps.

Hmm. Ron vibes mellow enough. Think I'll engage...

"It's kinda early to be finishing a shoot, isn't it?"

Ron,

"Well, It was a gang bang scene that went into the night."

(Crickets)

"I used to be kinda freaked out doing the whole S&M thing, but they teach you how to do it carefully. It's really all just for show.
Anyway, Kink was having a party on the roof of the Armory last night during the shoot and so I just stayed after for that."

I return,

"What's the deal with partying while working? Aren't you guys supposed to be sober on shoots these days?"

And Ron,

"Well, depends on what company you're doing the shoot for. Kink is a bunch of mellow hipsters. They're one of the ones who treat talent right and are cool, as long as it doesn't get out of hand.
They let people watch and party while talent stays sober. Bang Brothers in Florida kinda sucks though. Ft. Lauderdale's a different scene."

Ron continues under his breath,

"Bang Brothers has a couple spin-off gay sites, but they're *really* homophobic. Assholes."

And Ron moves seamlessly back on topic, and in full voice,

"Well, there *was* this one chick on the roof last night who was trying to get me drunk and fuck me, but I kept it cool."

Wait. Bang Brothers? Spin-off "gay sites"?

I pursue,

"So, you do gay porn, too? Are you bi in your personal life? If you don't mind my asking..."

Ron doesn't mind,

"Well, I got curious when I was nineteen and answered an ad on Craigslist from an older man. I think it was just the whole forbidden fruit thing about it. I never told any of my girlfriends, except for the bi one. She didn't care, though. I still cheated on her with guys, too. Then, I joined the Marines."

(Okay...)

I flounder,

"Wow. Did you see action? Er, how was it being gay in the Marines? I mean, I can see it flying in the Air Force... so to speak"

Ron,

"Oh, I never went to war. I was just stationed in North Carolina working a motor pool. You kind of expect to be shipped out the whole time and even *want* to go off to war for the bragging rights and street cred and all, whatever you might think about the politics.

Anyway, you still hook-up with other gay Marines through Craigslist, just off base is all. It's not a problem. Happens a lot. It's gotten kind of old for me now, though."

And,

"Anyway, I got a less-than-honorable discharge before I could get rotated abroad."

(Huh?)

"Uh, really?"

And Ron,

"Yeah, I had a problem with alcohol. They kicked me out after the sixth incident, when I fell off a roof and landed flat on my back. My buddies all thought I was dead, but I didn't even break anything. Don't remember any of it though.

Funny thing is, they didn't kick me out when I beat up a bunch of North Carolina police in a bar; maybe cause my superior liked me.

Anyway, he said I could appeal the discharge decision and try to get my benefits back. College would be cool, but I don't see how I'd win."

I move on,

"Hey! Do you know anything about the owner of Kink getting arrested for coke a few months ago? I read about how there was something in a shoot that aired online that led the cops to getting a warrant and busting-in and arresting dude after finding his stash!"

Ron,

"Yeah, I was *there*! It was surreal, like in a movie. A whole S.W.A.T. team kicked-in the doors and secured the Armory running around with assault rifles and shit!"

<u>Aside</u>: Ok. How ironic is it that a S.W.A.T. team kicks-in the doors of the San Francisco Armory to bust a bondage porn site housed there?

"They saw a handgun that belonged to the owner being discharged in one of the films online, and they came to bust him for that. But they only found his coke."

We eventually arrive at SFO - Delta, and Ron hands me up a Kink.com Citizen's Cab voucher pre-filled and made out for $45.
He then adds $3 cash to the pot of his own money as extra tip. Good guy.

I thank Ron and wish him well. And Ron does likewise... as he offers up his hand to shake!

Uhhhh. Shit.

With strained smile, I hide a cringe and everything suddenly goes all s l o w motion as I extend my hand in return, to shake...

We do, and we part.

11am:

Despite the airport, I still can't shake the feeling I'm playing catch-up from this morning. But I *have* actually accepted several Cabulous mobile-to-mobile hails *and* dispatched orders, too. And I have found hope - despite most of these proving short rides. The Cabulous default set 20% tip on the mobile orders *is* proving helpful, anyway.

I'm up in Potrero Hill when,

"Cha-ching! – 2601 48th Ave. Dispatch."

I 'Accept', without thinking.

<u>Note</u>: Drivers can 'Decline' an order. But subcontracted or no, it earns a driver no favors with Citizen's to not "play the radio", or so warned Jesus. Retribution could mean anything from getting bad cabs, to a bad schedule, to getting passed over on airport orders.

Wait. This order's like twenty minutes across town by way of the highway, over behind S.F. State! Why am I being sent this call? Is this normal? Surely, some other driver is closer.

Then, Kojak comes over the radio,

"722. Thanks for getting this. No flags, 722. These people need to get to the airport. Can you make it in fifteen minutes?"

"Uh, 722. I'll sure try. Thanks!"

Fifteen minutes later...

Okay! Bat outta hell, I'm almost there. Only gonna be like *two* minutes late.

I 'Call Passenger' through the Cabulous phone to let 'em know.

Voicemail. Damn.

Ok. I'll see if Kojak has any luck getting through. I reach for the CB handset.

But before I can speak, Kojak comes over the radio first with,

"722, put your brakes on. Put your brakes on. Your order just cancelled."

Fuuuck!

"722. Copy. They musta known I was close."

Great. I bet they totally called multiple cab companies. Another huge waste of time. I'm sure they must totally have a hard time getting cabs to come for them out this far, but now *I'm* out on the edge of town and twenty minutes away from any realistic hope of a street flag or dispatch. Ugh.

(Is this the part where I'm supposed to be seeing only one set of footprints in the sand?)

OOOoooMMMmmm.

Noon:

I'm heading into the Mission from a SOMA drop and I'm stopped at a red at Division, under the 101 on-ramp.

Figure I'll continue cruising straight up Mission and eventually take the right on 18th passing the hipster-French-bakery-and-sustainable-food-market block and on toward the Castro - if I don't catch a flag along the way first.

If my strategy proves, um, organically-unfruitful, then it's on toward the Haight.

But suddenly at the red here, a slightly haggard-looking blonde in a fuzzy tan low cut dress accessorized with a wide gaudy rhinestone-studded belt sheepishly approaches my half-opened shotgun window and bends in jiggling, betraying two pock-mock-scarred smallish tits. (She looks probably 30, but looks almost 50.)

The small-tittied Anna Nicole half-smiles, and inquires all edgy in a rasp,

"You open?"

"Uhhh. Guess so," I return, caught off guard and sensing something afoul (other than the cheap and excessively-applied fruity-smelling perfume).

"Okay! Pull over and wait here! I got a couple bags! I'll be right back!"

And with this, Anna Nicole runs off toward the low-rent storage facility at the corner here behind where she hailed me. (I know it's low rent, cause Christian - of Spermula fame - has a unit here. And Christian's as thrifty as they come.)

Wait... Storage space? Couple bags? Hmmm.

Whatever.

I pull over and Anna Nicole does indeed come right back, all hunched over dragging a big black duffel bag with one arm and an overstuffed Hefty bag with the other.

I unbuckle to go to help and just motion to pop the trunk (though I don't surmise this an airport). But Anna Nicole has already opened her door and started cramming her unwieldy bags into the back seat.

Whatever.

Huffing heavily, Anna Nicole squeezes in next to her bags and comes out with,

"Give me a second. I'll figure out where we're going. Just wait a minute. No! Actually, can you drive?"

Clipboard on steering wheel and pen in hand,

"Uhhh. Should I go straight down Mission? Or turn right on Division here?" (Blowing off the same Rose Commandment for the second time in two days of "Thou Shalt not drive without first being provided a destination".)

(Crickets)

Screw it.

I start down Mission before gently and s l o w l y pursuing my previous line of questioning,

"Uh, just where are you *going*. What is it you're *trying to do*?"

Still gasping for breath, Anna Nicole starts-in in her gravelly voice,

"I'm having the WORST day of my life!"

(Well, yes. I'd say "life possessions in a Hefty bag" are a sure sign of "bad day".)

Okay... How to respond?

"Uh, really?" is all I can come up with. (Sorry.)

But Anna Nicole doesn't care. She goes on,

"You DON'T know!"

"I've been hanging out in the hall outside my storage space since last night trying to charge my phone, but it won't charge! And I came to pay the late fee on my unit and I thought that'd let me back in, but you gotta pay the whole late rent too! And my boyfriend just broke-up with me and HE TOOK MY DEBIT CARD!!"

(Wait. She better have cash…)

Then, Anna Nicole breaks like the St. Francis Dam, crying HARD and sniffling something awful,

"And no hotels will let me in without a credit card!! I tried the Francisco and they're full up!! Do you know any hotels that will let me stay without a credit card?"

"Uhhh. I dunno. I think most want one? Uh…"

And the ensuing flood,

"WWwwwWW-AAAaaAA-HHhhhhHHH!!!!!"

(Well, hmm. The Francisco is a shitty hotel one level up from San Francisco's ubiquitous crack head Single Resident Occupancies, a.k.a. S.R.O. hotels.)

I start to think…

And ignoring the fact that there's a strange homeless chick in my back seat uncontrollably sobbing, I offer in a buoyant tone,

"Oh, yeah! What about the Oasis, or the Roadway Inn? They might take you without a credit card."

(The kids and I are unfortunately all too acquainted with these two "hotels" from a couple years ago, when "clients" of the Red Cross.)

It turns out that Anna Nicole has already tried the Road Rat, but not the Oasis...
We drive.
Then Anna Nicole breaks from the waterworks (a little bit) with,

"Hey, can I use your phone to call some hotels? Do you get 411 for free? (Sniff, sniff.)"

"Uh, I don't know if I get 411 for free. Uh..."

Jeez. Am I just gonna drive Anna Nicole around randomly for hours waiting outside as she checks random hotels to see if they'll let her stay without a credit card? And *then* hope she can pay the probable $100 plus fare at the end... IN CASH?

Ugh.

And, wait...

Is this a scam to steal my phone? Is she just gonna jump out at the next red?

Guess not. Can't run too fast while dragging all her life's possessions.

"Uh, sure. You can use my phone."

"Thanks! Never mind 411. I'll just make a local call. (Sniff, sniff.)"

Anna Nicole makes her call, and gets voicemail. She leaves a short incoherent message for her ex asking about her debit card.

Then it is decided: If the Oasis won't accept her without a credit card, we'll continue on up Franklin to the strip of touristy hotels on Lombard in the Marina.

En route, I conclude a change in subject is in order. I start-in with talking about how my kids and I stayed at the Road Rat... er, Rodeway Inn and then the Oasis after the crack dealers living in the flat below us burned us out of our building after sponsoring their third annual fire. (They got better at it with each consecutive year.)

And with this Anna Nicole continues to calm, settling down to only mild waterworks now and a light sniffle ensconced in my tale and visibly beaming at the thought of kids.

She apologizes for crying.

And now smiling, she thanks me for the distraction of my story, before adding that I have a "good vibe".

I return with a casual (and relieved) "no problem", following up with the assurance that "everything will be ok". I cap it all with a "just focus on what your next moves are". (Uh, huh.)

Guess a bed would be first on that list.

So, we exit the Mission, cross Market and start up Franklin toward the Oasis. I now begin to think that maybe my plan is a bad one. And wonder what I can do to help the poor girl out while moving on a little sooner to a fare that's ACTUALLY GOING TO PAY ME! Hmmm.

"Hey! Ya know, if the Oasis is no good, maybe I can drop you at the Main Library at Civic Center, and you can use the internet there to find a hotel."

(I have a homeless musician friend who frequents San Francisco's Main Library. And he is not the only one.)

But Anna Nicole is having none of it,

"Nah, can't drag my bags around the library. But, hey! You gave me an idea! Let's try the Civic Center Inn! It's close and they might let me stay!"

And she continues, pondering aloud,

"I hear the bass from the strip club next door can keep you up at night, but that might be fun."

So, we divert from heading to the Oasis to the seedy bowels of the Tenderloin; home of the (misnomered) Civic Center Inn.

Then, a light bulb!

"Hey! I know a lot of cab drivers stay at the Elk. It's next to The Civic Center Inn. Actually, there's like ten places in the Tenderloin there that are all probably cool about no credit card! Is it ok if I just drop you off at the Civic Center Inn and you can maybe walk around to check out the others if you need to? I mean, this ride could get expensive and it sounds like you should be watching your money."

And... She buys it!

"Well, I guess maybe they'll let me leave my bags in the lobby while I walk around, if they don't let me stay. Sure. Okay!"

<u>Of note</u>: The Civic Center Inn is also conveniently caddie corner to a homeless shelter.

We pull up to Ellis & Polk, and Anna Nicole gets out lugging her bags behind her to the sidewalk before coming back over and once again bends-in to the shotgun window all jiggling and beginning to nervously sort though some cash.

She notes the meter on the dash reads $11.55 and with shaky hands, Anna Nicole forks over a crumpled ten and two ones. She apologizes profusely for leaving "no tip" before adding a neurotic,

"I'm sure other people will make it up to you. You have such good karma."

I am emphatic that she not worry about me or the tip and reiterate that she should just focus on getting herself a bed, before offering another "it'll all be ok".

At with this, Anna Nicole looks me deep in the eyes and playfully cocks her head again half-smiling, and thanks me.

And Anna Nicole goes hunching off dragging her two overstuffed bags behind her past the crack dealers on the corner, and into the office of the Civic Center Inn.

The rest of the day plays out with a decent amount of homogenous young white techie local runs. But it all adds up. And thank Buddha!

At E.O.D. back at the lot, Jesus is working the window. I hand in my Kink voucher, Paratransit receipts and cash, etc. through the tray under the bullet-proof glass. And only then do I ask Jesus half-heartedly if there's any down-time I can cash-in on for working the 1064 accident. Indeed, he says I was marked down for 30 dollars off my gate.

Sweet Jesus! Yes!

He returns back thirty through the tray in light of the reduced $75 gate and I tip him $5 before he hands me my receipt, and a snack pack of raisins.

I thank Jesus, and turn to leave.

My third day on the job and I somehow eked out a $194 walk.

It seems I now have a career.

OM.

Chapter 6

Thursday
People
Need
A
Ride...

The infamous Milford is working the office and throws me 744, a Camry he describes as "new" with a 5 o' clock medallion. I throw him a five and he looks disappointed and expectant. I ignore this. Why am I gonna tip him more for this?

I head out to the lot, prep the cab, report some bumper marks over the radio to cover my ass, then proceed to leave the lot.

Suddenly, the Dutchman (a mellow, eccentric, 64 year-old driver who looks 50 and lives two hours away in the Santa Cruz mountains where he has local girls trained as his personal prostitutes) has me roll down my window and asks where I'm going.

I ask him where he's going, if he needs a ride.

He says 744 is *his* cab...

"What? Milford gave me 744," I reply.

But the Dutchman just drawls back, "Milford's crazy."

We both head back to the office to sort it out and Milford whines that the Dutchman's not on the list today, but gives him 744 anyway and hands me 330, which has a 3:30 medallion. Extra tip indeed.

I head out for real now.

It's slow again this morning and I've been feeling competitive. It's stressful and juvenile, but I give in to it. It might be that I'm currently caught up with money and debts, and without that there's nothing left to look forward to or distract me. I have arrived at the center of the onion.

I've found that being a cab driver offers nothing more in terms of life goals than looking for a fare, and/or completing a bagged fare in the very short term. But this is what I signed up for, and want. This is my sand mandala.

If there's one thing I took from 9/11, it's the sight of all those papers from the World Trade Center flying around. What do spreadsheets and memos mean at the end of the day? Nothing.

I recently sent my Ma a good new recording of my band Spermula. All of our music is completely off the cuff and we never actually write (and consequently never repeat) a song. Very apt.

Ma, not surprisingly, did not like the heavy, angry music (all the songs lately have been about Christian's ex who screwed him up good).

Ma said,

"Where are you going with this 'music'?"

Going?

Where is there to go? Where am I, or anyone, "going" with anything? Ultimately, to the grave.

Dad taught me that a man's worth in life is measured by what he's done for society; well, people need a ride...

6:48am:

My younger boy's going to a week-long overnight outdoor education trip with the rest of his elementary school class. It's a place called Foothill Horizons near Yosemite. They're meeting now with their bags outside his school in the Marina. His mom had him last night and I'm going to try and catch him at school to say my last goodbye for a few days. I'll miss him.

I pass a flag along the way, but my boy's worth it.

Once there, I pick him up and shake and hug him and kiss him all over his face, despite his attempts to thwart me. I'm embarrassing him.

As I go to leave, I find another of my son's classmate's parents double-parked in front of the school with their car hood up and dad sporting jumper cables.

I don't know them. But they ask me for a jump and I graciously oblige.

Once my cab's hood is up, we have trouble discerning which terminal is positive and which is negative. Chang finally says he's sure which is which and I nervously let him do his business. (Security deposit?)

CHUG... CHUG... CHUG... VRRROOOOM!

Whew! Chang and wife thank me and I'm on my way! Off to the morning Marina hunt! (Marina = white collar financial types with disposable income.)

9:15am:
"Cha-ching! - 2407 Webster. Dispatch." Cool enough. I'm close. And this is from dispatch. I'll earn some points.

I 'Accept'.

I get there fast and out pops a jittery-but-nice dyke in a tweed blazer. It seems Ellen is late getting to her lawyer's to entertain an insurance settlement from Traveller's. It's been a three-year battle since her building caught fire, due to a dollar store extension cord her landlord put too much load on.

She tells me her dog died in the fire and she lost all her blazers, except for the one she's wearing.

So, Ellen goes on to say she only shops at the Salvation Army now and for a period after the fire was a client of the Red Cross. They set her up in a hotel for a while and gave her money, etc.

I relay that I too was once a post-fire client of the Red Cross and we bond about how great they are.

Anyway, it seems Traveller's has the worst reputation for drawing out settlements and wearing you down. I get her to her appointment in the Financial - Montgomery & Bush - pretty fast (but about ten minutes late) and we part warmly with me $15 richer.

Noon:
"Cha-ching! 1300 Laguna. Dispatch." I'll take it.

This is near the Western Addition projects though, and likely a short ride.

I get there and 'Call Passenger'.

Shortly, a 50-something white woman comes out followed by a 20-something pretty girl with Betty Page bangs, in slippers, PJs and covered in a blanket. She's got a hospital wrist band on and betrays freshly scabbed cut marks on her wrist... across, not along the vein.

They get in and in a European accent, mom asks me to take them to the Rodeway Inn.

Hey! The Road Rat! Where the kids and I stayed after *our* fire! (Well, our neighbors.) When *we* were "clients" of the Red Cross. Serendipity.

It was weird. One night I had the 'Do Not Disturb' sign on the door and the dude who runs the place walked in on me naked without knocking. I yelled at him and he ran out. The next morning when I was checking-out there was an older couple checking in. I told them to watch out for the "pervert desk dude". I warned the couple right in front of him, too. He proceeded to lie about having walked in on me, then changed his story when pressed to say he thought our room was leaking water from the bathtub. We hadn't even used the shower or tub yet. Right. Freak.

Anyway, The Road Rat is only 6 blocks straight up Eddy. Pbbbbttt! Short ride, indeed.

So, the fare ends up to at $5.15 and mom starts going through her purse and counting pennies. She gives me five ones and fifteen pennies <u>exactly</u>. And no tip.

Fuckin' Europeans. This is America. You play by our rules when coming here. That's just rude. No wonder Betty Page is so fucked up.

Later…

N.P.R.'s doing a forum on some Google privacy policy as I'm picking up a lawyer woman in the Financial. I ask her what she thinks about the issue.

Miers informs me that half of all human resource managers check a potential employee's Twitter and Facebook accounts before hiring these days.

Nothing we discuss is really pertinent to whether Miers cares about being tracked via cookies or not when surfing the web, but she does go on to relay a strange internet experience she had not too long ago...

Seems Miers and family were trying to rent an apartment somewhere in Europe for vacation. And before agreeing, the renter had asked Miers for the names of everyone in her family, including her teenage son.

The guy did ultimately agree to rent the apartment to them, but before doing so asked in all seriousness that the son "not perform Kung Fu in the apartment".

It turns out her son had put up a silly mock Kung Fu video of himself and a friend sparring on YouTube some years ago.

Miers went on to say how it kinda freaked her out, the lengths to which she was investigated, and unnecessary request.

2:40pm:

I've got time for one more fare. And right on cue,

"Cha-ching! - 1981 Union. Lululemon. iPhone."

This one is NOT from dispatch. It's direct from someone's cell, a mobile order.

And, hmm. I'm up on Fillmore in Pac Heights and will likely catch a flag *here* at this time.

And my Cabulous suitor is on Union ten blocks away... with empty cabs going by every two seconds!

Should I take this?

Will the flag be there?

I reluctantly 'Accept' the call.

But I keep an open mind to cancelling for a flag, if my suitor doesn't cancel first!

I get as far as Union & Fillmore when I spot a Mexican dude trying to flag me at the corner.

But I'm close to Lululemon now and resign to following through.

I feel bad though. There's no way to turn off the top-light promoting me as "available", unless you turn on the meter. Jorge' probably thinks I'm dissing him. Oh, well.

I get to the corner of Union & Buchanan and a typical Cow Hollow chick is hailing me. But she's looking at her phone. It's my Cabulous flag! Watching me arrive on the real time map on her app. Heather gets in,

"SFO, please. And I'm late! I thought my flight was at 5, but it's at 4! Can we make it?"

Score!

She has no bags. I woulda never thought this was an airport. Guess I got good Karma for not cancelling on her.

I try to be positive and reassure Heather that since she's not checking a bag, I think we have a good chance of getting her to SFO in time for her flight. And Heather settles back in her seat and relaxes, with a soothing vibe.

I check her in the rear view...

She's nice. And kinda pretty. Hmm. Not typically "Cow Hollow". The "nice" and "soothing vibe" part that is.

Anyway, turns out Heather is flying up to Seattle to get her stuff and then drive back down to San Francisco. She's moving here and just secured a job at Lululemon.

Go yoga pants!

Heather and I eventually hit the straightaway on 101 south. We're passing Candlestick Park when all of a sudden all three lanes lock up. What the hell? It's not rush hour, yet.

Jesus is working at dispatch now and comes over the radio warning that the two right lanes on 101 south are closed due to an overturned car.

Shit.

Where was Jesus two minutes ago?? When I could have diverted to 280 south! Not only will Heather not make her flight now, but I'm also gonna be late back with the cab! And that's 15 bucks!

I radio-in to Jesus to tell him I'll likely be a little late back with the cab, as to warn the next driver.

Jesus thinks I'm asking him to rearrange things so that no one will be waiting for me back at Citizen's and says he'll do what he can, but "no promises".

That's not why I radioed him, but I do very much appreciate the effort.

Even if I do have to pay the night driver the 15 dollar late charge, this fare will likely land around 60 bucks and still make economic sense.

So, Heather and I eventually pass the accident and gawk at an overturned Mustang and a sideways-landed Jeep Cherokee amidst all the emergency vehicles and debris.

We're moving fast now. Heather might still make her flight. But I see my 101 northbound returning traffic sucks, due to rubbernecking. I'm gonna have to take 280 back, and pray.

I drop Heather at SFO in the nick of time - $60 richer, cash - and recklessly speed back up 280 north, quite successfully.

I resign myself to just hitting the expensive Amoco by the lot. Gotta cut my losses.

I fill the cab (at $100/gallon) and finally make into the Citizen's Cab lot at exactly 3:35pm, five minutes late. But...

No one is out front waiting!

Sweet!

I get up to the bullet-proof glass where I'm to check-out and find Milford working the window. (Jesus is still back on the radio at dispatch.)

Milford doesn't seem to realize there was a question of me being late and I realize Jesus has done nothing to help. I just got lucky that the night driver hasn't shown up yet.

I "Accept".

And walk with $210!

As I start to head out of the Citizen's lot, I note an animated scene up on the rustic porch by check-out and decide to stay a second and shoot the shit with some night drivers hanging out there.

The porch acts as a break room of sorts and sports a couch and Coke machine up a few wooden steps under a corrugated plastic roof strewn with old top-lights about on top.

There's a night driver, Jack Daniel, up there giving the stories to an avid crowd. I quickly deduce him to be a man of great taste and refinement.

Jack is about my age. And he says at one time he was a tour manager for some pretty big-time thrash/hardcore bands.

Hey! It seems we probably crossed paths back in the day when my band Dicksister opened up for D.R.I. at the old 9:30 Club in D.C.!

Jack comes across as easy, quick-witted and refreshingly un-PC… and he *gets away* with it.

Also doubling as a dispatcher, Jack's buoyant charms seem to afford him leeway to address female callers-in as "honey", and even woo them in so doing! (I've queried a couple dispatched female passengers on this and survey says it's all about *how* you say "honey".)

So, after some various music talk, Jack lays his best cab story on me. It goes a little something like this…

It was a dark and stormy night. And Jack's out cruising the Mission for fares when out pops a pretty 20-something blonde. He pulls over, and 'Accepts'.

A somber Ashley gets in back, and directs our boy to her abode in the Castro, before retreating back into a melancholy silence.

But a social Jack, post feeling-out the sitch, quickly cracks the façade and gets Ashley to talking.

They hit it off over the short ride to 17th & Sanchez and Jack is triumphant in lifting Ash's spirits.

Once at drop, a now energized Ashley pays the meager fare, pauses, and grins all Cheshire-like with an offer,

"Hey. You wanna come upstairs?"

(Well. Far be it for Jack to be rude.)

"Ok."

Once up in Ashley's flat, she gets right to business dropping to her knees just inside the doorway, and violently unlocks Jack's chastity belt before diving full-on into a truly earnest blow job.

("Best tip I ever had," Jack tells me.)

So, Jack cums in her mouth and Ashley smiles broadly.
She forgoes any request of reciprocation for sprightly inquiring,

"Hey! Can you take me back to where you picked me up in the Mission and wait for me?"

Jack, a little unsure of the impetus here and sensing something amiss, puts away any hesitation and simply shrugs,

"Sure. Why not?"

(At this point in the story, I have to ask Jack if he turned the meter on for the return trip. He asserts unflinchingly, "Of course I did!")

So, Ash and Jack drive back toward her original pick-up on Valencia in the Mission with an excited Ash bubbling in back.

At this point, our boy is starting to wonder what he's gotten himself into. If Ash's marbles are all in one place.

Once on Valencia, she jumps out of the cab gleefully with,

"Thanks for waiting! I'll be right back!"

And Jack hunkers down.

Five minutes later....

Ash runs back out, and jumps in the cab bursting at the seams as she blurts out,

"Take me back home!!"

Jack is now convinced a few marbles are indeed M.I.A.

After about a minute of silence, with Jack checking the rear view periodically to witness a giddy Ashley, she finally lets loose,

"I just broke up with my boyfriend!!"

So, Jack acknowledges this information nervously with a simple, "Uh-huh," wondering if *he* is now her boyfriend...

But Ash goes on,

"Ya know how when you first picked me up how I was sad? Well, I went to surprise my boyfriend at his apartment, but found him fucking my best friend on his couch! He didn't see me and I ran outside freaking just before hailing you."

And she continues,

"Anyway, I had you drive me back to break up with him. But we made-out super hot and heavy first before I told him. Boy was *he* surprised! I can't believe it. He even tried to deny cheating on me! I told him, 'Don't fuck with me! I saw you two on the couch! I'M BREAKING UP WITH YOU!'"

And Ashley caps,

"'Oh, and by the way... HOW DOES MY CAB DRIVER TASTE?!'"

Chapter 7

Friday
Road Closed?

4:50am:

It's the last day of my first week driving a cab. And I live!

Well, almost. I haven't had coffee yet.

But I am done yawning through the office and dispatch morning bribe ritual.

I head to my cab, 561 - a Ford Fusion with a 5 'o clock medallion.

She's parked next to a Filipino driver's cab who's also sporting a Fusion today.

In deference to C.Y.A., we both inspect our cabs for low tire pressure and any unreported damage that could potentially get pinned on us (and thereby cost us our security deposits).

I jokingly ask Marcos if his cab actually *started* this morning, or if he had to do the Fusion song and dance.

The one I've seen other drivers cursing their way through a couple mornings this week.

This is when the Fusion locks you out as a suspected thief and you have to stow the key somewheres twenty or more yards away from the cab, and then wait five minutes before coming back and trying to start it again. The dance does seem to work. But jeez.

Thankfully, I haven't had to deal with the infamous Fusion starting problem, yet. But I've come to learn keeping low expectations is the smart way to go in this business. And I have not been disappointed. Anyway, the Fusion check is surely in the mail.

It was kinda crazy watching a driver deal with one of these lockouts earlier in the week, when he was sent right out of the office running with an overdue airport order (way across town, of course).

So, Marcos confirms his Fusion did start today. But goes on to say how it did lock him out yesterday while he was washing his cab. Marcos says that the Fusions "have ghosts in them".

Side Note: I don't get the whole "washing the cab" thing. I've been cleaning the inside pretty good thus far, but who really cares what they look like out?

5:40am:

I'm post-morning routine, and it's slow…

I've been through the Mission, Castro, Upper

and Lower Haights, the Fillmore and Pac Heights.

Nothing.

It's still early, but this affords *way* too much time to think, introspect, and ruminate on about how you're just spinning your wheels... er, so to speak.

To add further to this feeling of foreboding, I have been following only empty cabs going *to* where I am going, and finding only empty cabs coming *from* where I'm going to!

Still, S.F. *is* a beautiful town; however quiet.

I make it all the way to Cow Hollow sans-fare when,

"Cha-ching! -1803 Broadway. Dispatch."

I definitely 'Accept'.

Time to break the ice!

I was "rolling bingo" (coincidentally at the order) when it was called over the radio and hence, I easily won the call. Straightaway, I pull into the drive.

I 'Call Passenger' and wait.

In short order, out pops a 20-something girl comfortably dressed in yoga pants and slightly disheveled.

It seems she's only going a short distance to Sacramento & Steiner. This is not far, situated on just the other side of this well-off part of San Francisco, in Pac Heights.

My sense is that she's just returning home from a

night at her boyfriend's (or boyfriend for a night).

This is a first for me. And it feels kinda weird to be driving someone home from a booty call so early in the morning.

So, O.K. Cupid and I ride in silence and the ride culminates in me $10 richer, via credit card of course. It's a small fare, but "all good" as they say. I'm just happy the day has finally begun.

Think I'll head back over toward Cow Hollow again. It's my best chance for a flag this early. I can probably score a Financial shuttle headed to 555 Cal (Bank of America), or maybe a day tripper headed to the airport.

One added bonus of cruising the Union Street strip down there has been checking out what young hotties might be working-out at the Crunch gym at this time.

The Union Street branch has two levels to it with a big glass front wall that works to a voyeur's advantage when it's still dark out, as it is now.

All the local yuppie bottle blondes in yoga pants are there pre-work, jiggling on the stair climbers with ponytails swaying seductively side to side.

Of note: The Crunch on Chestnut in the adjacent Marina district and seems to exhibit an older, flabbier post-kid clientele. (What? I'm a man!)

I don't know what it is. I'm not attracted to prostitutes. (Too gaudy.) But Cow Hollow's painted pretties with their dyed hair, yoga pants and copious amounts of make-up *do* somehow turn my head. (This, despite a mental aversion to the farce.)

I know most of them aren't as pretty as they *look*. But try telling this to my libido. Someone didn't get the memo.

Hmm. Maybe it's their narcissism, or the thing of wanting what you can't have. Dunno.

7:30am:

I'm driving up Polk just passing Broadway, and a 20-something chick jumps out from the sidewalk vehemently flagging me. She looks a little distraught. I pull over.

"The court house at Beale & 6th, please."

"Uhhh. There is no courthouse on Beale, or 6th."

(*And* these two streets are parallel. Hey! I'm getting good!)

"Oh! 850 *Bryant*. Not Beale. Sorry! I'm picking up my car. It was towed."

"That sucks. AutoReturn it is."

And I continue with a need to know,

"So. What happened?"

"Arggg. I lent my car to my sister last night and it somehow got loose after she parked it. They said it rolled down the street and landed on the sidewalk!"

"Wow. That sucks," I respond with a valiant display of empathy.

As we near AutoReturn (which is actually at 7th & Bryant) coming down 8th Street, I pass a guy with luggage trying to flag me at Folsom.

(It's weird how often people try to flag you when you're full.)

I sigh and wave him off, but *do* take note the intersection.

Dude might have a hard time getting a cab there at this time. 8th *and* Bryant are both one-way streets en route to downtown. Most cabs on these fast-moving streets will likely be full already, as I am.

But the courthouse and tow lot (a.k.a. Autoreturn) is only a couple blocks away. And post-drop, I zoom back for my airport!

Adrenalin no friend, I have to waste precious time doing several one-way street dances through SOMA down here to get back to 8th & Folsom. But the Traffic Light Gods bless me and I'm back to where dude was flagging in no time. And…

He's still there!

"SFO – United, please."

Sweet!

First airport of the day. We ride in silence.

8:15am:

I'm on 101 north coming back from dude's SFO when,

"Cha-ching! - 50 Shawnee. Dispatch."

I 'Accept'. But I have to rely on the Cabulous GPS to find this one. It's one of those orders in the netherworld I hear dispatchers trying to unload over the radio, by fishing for drivers coming back from the airport. Cab drivers don't frequent the outskirts of San Francisco. It's a sea of single family homes, residential districts. They have cars. And they don't have money for cabs.

Yeah, these are orders that you'd otherwise pass along the highway returning from SFO if you weren't "playing the radio". A lot of times these people (when they do call) can end up waiting for up to an hour for a cab.

So, I jump off of 101 north and divert onto 280 south, per GPS. And I make it to 50 Shawnee in like five minutes to find my fare; a middle-aged slightly haggard-looking white woman smoking a cigarette with a cat carrier on her lap. She's been outside sitting on her porch waiting for me.

Turns out Rosanne is headed to a pet hospital in the Mission. We get to talking...

It seems her cat of fifteen years, Twinkle, has cancer and is now going in for a follow-up on a mastectomy.

Wow. I didn't know cats *got* mastectomies.

Rosanne then changes the subject by lamenting aloud about how I'm the second cab to come for her. Apparently, dispatch called her work phone number when the first taxi came and the driver didn't bother to get out of the cab to ring the bell.

Doh!

The driver was advised to leave after Tupac the dispatcher tried calling and got voice mail.

Anyway, I go on to tell Roseanne that I've heard Jesus, Citizen's Cab's manager, give drivers crap over the radio for not getting off their asses to ring the door bell. (The CB radio banter has actually been quite entertaining this week.)

Anyway, Rosanne says she called Tupac and bitched him out over the whole deal. Wow.

In light of this, I attempt a fall on the Citizen's sword and offer Rosanne the ride free. But she just laughs the offer off with,

"That's alright, Honey. We still got time."

I do indeed get Rosanne to the pet hospital on time, and she throws me a twenty.

God bless Rosanne, and Twinkle!

10:15am:

I feel a dead period coming on (as I've found is

not unusual for this time of day).

Tupac is calling out "19th Avenue & Lake" over the radio. And no one is biting.

Hmm. I'm in the Marina, but I *could* cut through the Presidio from here. I probably should be securing a ride about now. I'd also be scoring points for "playing the radio".

I radio-in,

"561. Lombard & Divis. I'll travel…"

"Thank you, 561," Tupac comes back.

And he sends me the order proper to my Cabulous phone with a "Cha-ching!"

Who knows? Maybe it'll be a good ride. Probably isn't going too close to home all the way out there anyway.

I get to 19ᵗʰ & lake after a serene and scenic eight minute ride through the Presidio, basking in the view of the wide open Pacific and Golden Gate Bridge.

I 'Call Passenger'.

And after a bit, a very old woman dressed for town (a bit on the purple side) comes slowly out,

"Chase Bank, at 19th & Noriega, please."

And we're off.

It's a no-brainer; straight down Park Presidio which soon becomes 19th Avenue. A straight shot, and a fast one at that.

Park Presidio is a three lane (each way) thoroughfare that cuts right through the middle of Golden Gate Park, and with very few lights.

So, halfway there Great Grandma breaks radio silence. She slowly leans forward, and softly speaks…

"*Where* are you going?"

Umm, wha??? Did I miss something? Is she senile?

I *re*-confirm our destination,

"Chase Bank, at 19th & Noriega. Right?"

(Crickets)

…

And *still* no reply.

We continue on, with a now awkward silence filling the cab.

We arrive at Chase within a couple minutes more, *both* pretending no question of route (or destination?) has been posed.

And Great Grandma hands me a Paratransit card

for the $9.55 ride.

I 'Add' the municipally-fixed 10% tip. And Great Grandma thanks me as she exits the cab.

Whew!

Whatever.

11:48-11:52am:

I'm driving east down Market and passing Westfield Mall when a white-trash looking dude with a gym bag jumps out in front of the cab at a red at 5th Street.

In a southern gravel evocative of Kid Rock, dude yells through the windshield asking if I'm open.

Rock is missing teeth, has freshly scabbed welts on his face and visually reeks of vagrant. I do hesitate, but gamble signaling him in as I wonder,

"What am I getting myself into?"

Rock opens the back door and throws in his gym bag, all the while complaining vociferously about how heavy it is.

Then, Rock shuts the back door and tries getting in front.

No!

Rose Commandment!! Rose Commandment!!

(And I am LISTENING this time!)

I have my whole office on the shotgun seat: my clipboard, my map book, a washcloth, bottle of water, and my Spermula CD. All very conspicuously arranged... and *still* Rock tries!

I physically push Rock back as he tries *three times* to obliviously sit on my stuff!

And each time I yell,

"Get in back, *please.*"

Rock finally realizes, and shuffles stumbling in back.

Rock speaks,

"Boyy. I suure glad I 'n Saan Fraancisco. Jus cam frum Saante Barbra. Suks dere, maan. Thay jump'd mee n' didd thes!" (Rock points at his face.)

(I am remiss in pursuit of asking who "thay" wunt.)

And,

"Thay tuk alll mii muny, to. Taake mee too uh cheep hohtel."

Wait.

What?

Took all his money? This again??

Hmm. Well, he *is* going to a hotel. And I know just the area; 6th Street is just a couple blocks away.

6th Street is the South of Market hold-tight-to-your-cell-phone extension of the Tenderloin district.

Rock will feel right at home there in one of the S.R.O. hotels catering to San Francisco's many crack addicts, thieves and low-grade prostitutes.

All in all, Rock seems nice enough I should say (much like many of the grown-up children I met in jail at age 21, when I opted out of alcohol education in exchange for a weekend in jail for a D.U.I. penance).

Rock goes on to gush about the town. He certainly does seem happy to be in San Francisco, or at least away from "Saante Barbra" anyway.

"I un alcaholik. Jus get kiked off tha trayn. N I wunt drunk r nuthin!! Jus haad me onne glas uh win too slep! Tha conductr didt lik mee!" Rock expounds, shaking his head, "N' tha cahps wudnt lisen! I haad mee thre wiitness I aint dune nuthin. Bible onlee assk fer too."

We find a random crack hotel at 6th & Mission, *fast.* The fare ends up at $6.80 and Rock hands me two fives, and then quickly adds another. He thanks me and says to "kep et".

But the ride is not over. Seems Rock has an

affinity for me.

He stops, looks at me, and as though in afterthought starts-in with daring me to try and lift his gym bag.

I do not leave the driver's seat, but as Rock seems determined to again commiserate on its heft, I turn around and reach over the seat with one arm to try and lift the bag.

"Wow! That *is* heavy!" I relay, hoping this is the end of it. And it pretty much is.

Rock then stumbles away from the cab while yelling,

"Whar's tha hohtel??"

I signal Rock to look up. He's standing directly under a huge "Kean Hotel" sign.

"Ohhhh!" Rock grins a toothless grin, and bids me "Byye!"

Goodbye, Rock.

1:15pm:

Driving east down Market in the Financial, I'm hoping for a businessman day tripper airport, outgoing.

I make it almost to the end of Market when a suit with luggage does indeed flag me, from the wrong side of Market.

Shit.

I can't make a U-turn here... or can I?

Shit.

I give Suit a thumbs-up and straddling the double yellow, pull up a just bit to the intersection at Front and stop... poised for my illicit maneuver. (But only after scanning for cops, of course.)

I signal left, and wait for oncoming traffic to pass...

It does, and I *just* start to make my U.

But before I even cross the double yellow,

"CRACCK! WHUUMP!! TUMMMBBBLLE!!"

Oh my God!! WHAT THE FUCK?!?

It's a cyclist! I've collided with a cyclist! Flying up from behind me, on the double yellow on my left!!

Jeez! And in the middle of Market no less!

I hit the brakes immediately as Armstrong spills over the hood of my dead-stopped cab. I'm dazed. He's dazed.
And Armstrong tumbles landing right in the middle of Market as the next wave of traffic coming from the east fast approaches!!

Shit!

But thankfully, they see Armstrong and all come screeching to a halt.

Jesus!

I roll down the window and yell,

"Oh, my God! Are you OK??"

And Armstrong gets up, dusts himself off and starts surveying his body,

"I think so. I just lost another pair of pants again, though."

(Armstrong picks at a fresh hole in his khakis. Wait. "Again"?)

Then, before I can react more or get out of the cab, some random dude runs up to me in the intersection and hands my side view mirror in to me in through the driver's window.

Wha? I didn't even realize it broke off!

Shit. This is bad.

Shaking, Armstrong starts walking his bike to the caddy-corner sidewalk, while nursing his hand.

Damn.

I think his hand might be broken. That's probably what tore the mirror off!

So, I'm stopped in the middle of the Front & Market intersection smack down in the Financial and dazed with a situation. I yell over,

"Do you need me to pull over??"

And Armstrong confirms that I "probably should".

Duh. I quickly come to my senses, realizing that this was a stupid question.

For Citizen's sake if nothing else, we need to exchange info.

I take the illegal left to pullover (though probably moot now) and meet Armstrong by the sidewalk.

I get out of the cab with a pen and a couple Citizen's Cab receipts/business cards to exchange phone numbers and names, etc.

And Armstrong apologizes.

He says he shouldn't have been passing on my left and riding down the double yellow. (He's right. That *is* illegal, even for a bike.)

I likewise apologize with,

"Yeah, and I was taking an illegal U-turn, too."
And add, "Guess we *both* messed up."

Let the love fest ensue.

Wait…

Doh!

I should *not* have said that.

I feel genuinely bad about the whole thing. But I'm still dazed. And as a result, I'm being stupid.

In addition to prematurely admitting some kind of fault, I'm breaking Citizen's Cab protocol by not immediately alerting dispatch and filling out a full accident kit. Ugh.

Guess it's not too late for the kit. Ah, screw it. I'll just get the info they need.

So, Armstrong and I both apologize *again* at the curb, but this time sans reference to illegal U-turns.

And Armstrong comes across a real nice guy. He tries looking out for me, asking if we can handle this without me having to let Citizen's know.

While I very much appreciate his concern for my job, I wince at the broken side view mirror sitting on my shotgun seat, frown and shake my head with,

"Nooo, but thanks."

I wouldn't have tried to hide the incident anyway. *Sooo* not worth it.

That course of action would surely have bitten me in the ass, in the end (so to speak).

And now a crowd is gathering. Out from the rest of the mob, two Japanese women shuffle over gawking with their cell phones out, and assure Armstrong that they've just called an ambulance.

But Armstrong exclaims,

"No! Please cancel it. I don't need an ambulance! I can't afford it, anyway."

I hand Armstrong my filled-out info, and then my pen and a Citizen's card for him to put down his. He takes the pen in his shaking hand and tries to write, but can't finish his chicken scratch. Damn.

Armstrong's hand is in too much pain, and he can't grip. Fuck.

He asks me to finish writing for him via dictation.

I do and once done, I ask Armstrong if he needs anything.

He simply says "no". And I wish him well, *again* apologize and tell him to call me with anything he may need.

Still loopy, I thoughtlessly go to shake his hand as Armstrong hesitates. But we shake.

He grimaces and I notice more how his hand is pretty scraped up. But Armstrong doesn't scream in pain during the shake. Still, I'm pretty sure it's broken. Damn.

Ugh!

I head to 101 south from downtown and back toward the lot, side-view mirror riding shotgun.

This is hampering me, especially while still dazed and now on the highway. But I drive *real* s l o w and real careful and don't change lanes. And I get away with it.

I make it to the cheap generic gas station on Cesar Chavez near the lot and gas it up.

Hmm. Think I'll call Christian for his thoughts and advice on this…

And Christian answers!

But he admonishes me big-time for copping to the attempted illegal U at the scene, and for not *immediately* calling dispatch and filling out a full accident kit. Damn. He's right.

I hang up and call Tony, who's now working dispatch.

Tony sounds shocked that I've left the scene without alerting him, or doing the full kit. It's not his problem, but his alarm is not a good sign.

Tony goes on to relent, groaning,

"Oh, well. Bring it in."

I'm soon pulling into the Citizen's lot with 561 and find Tony out by the porch smoking a cigarette.

I relay my story and ask what he thinks.

Tony sounds real dire about the whole thing and raises his eyebrows and says to "expect the worst".

Ugh.

"Hitting pedestrians is *bad*," he says, "But I don't want to put words in anyone's mouth. I dunnooo."

Tony shakes his head and exhales.

I pursue,

"Do I have to worry about being put "Out of Service" by Citizen's? Or being written out of the policy by the insurance company?"

"Both," he shoots back.

Great.

I go inside, and head to the *back* office to see Karen in admin and fill out a report. This one's mine.

I pass Jesus along the way, who just shakes his head looking stressed and avoiding eye contact.

Shit.

I see Karen and we head out to 561 together. She says she needs to pull the camera's memory card and take pictures of any damage the cab may have incurred (e.g., the side view).

Karen heads first for the camera inside the cab as

she notes aloud,

"The main chip looks bad. But the backup should
have something on it."

What? Backup chip?

Once done, we head again to the back office and
I finish filling out a report in the conference room –
where only a week ago I had orientation.

And there I write alone, behind closed doors, and
sweating.

I play it vague on the insurance report and omit
any apology to Armstrong.

When done, I head to the Xerox machine outside
of Karen's office to make myself a copy.

And as I'm doing so, Dave Hanes (owner of
Citizen's Cab) just then emerges from his office, as
Karen pops out from hers to intercept and update
Dave.

Caught in the middle in the hall there, I try to
make light of the situation in relaying half-jesting of
the cyclist,

"Well, he's still alive."

But Dave fails to see the humor and retorts with a
confused,

"What??"

Doh! Dave doesn't get that in my own way, I'm
just trying to say that Armstrong isn't hurt *too* bad.

I do go on to successfully communicate to Dave about Armstrong's hand though.

Damn.

So, Karen and I head back into the conference room for an oral debriefing.

I admit to her that I was going to make an illegal U, but add that Armstrong also admitted that he should not have been riding down the double yellow, and trying to pass on my left.

And Karen goes on to ask *how* I know that the turn is illegal,

"Are there signs?"

"Uhhh. I don't remember," but offer that it's common knowledge that there are no legal turns for most of Market downtown. And that I'm sure there are signs.

Karen continues,

"Did you actually *make* the U-turn? Or leave your lane?"

I think before replying,

"Uh, no. I never got that far."

Karen comes back,

"Well, then you didn't break the law."

She then adds,

"You never told me about the turn."

I reply simply,

"I love you."

I go on to ask if I'm "Out of Service" and Karen says that's up to Dave and the insurance company.

And, "Dave will be in to talk with you in a minute."

She then goes off into Dave's office in an adjacent room and I can hear them talking all muffled through the conference room wall.
Soon enough, Dave does come into the conference room and proceeds very serious.
I keep it cool and just answer his questions directly, without emoting…

Dave: "Have you had any accidents in the last year?

Me: "Well, no. I'm kinda new at Citizen's."

Dave: "Good. When our new insurance company looks it up, the first thing they'll see is number of accidents."

Me: "Okay..."

Dave: "As it is, we are on a thread with them."

Me: "Yeah, I heard."

(There's been some gab about Citizen's having a new insurance company and the subsequent slew of driver's names put up on the Out of Service whiteboard at dispatch.)

Dave (surprised): "You have? Well, it looks like you were not at fault here. We'll see if the cyclist tries to make a claim. We do have to go ahead and submit the report to the insurance company, regardless. We'll see what happens. But for now if you want to get a spare and go back out, you can."

Wha??

Yes!

And Dave gets up to leave the room and I am grateful, but decline the spare,

"Thanks, but I probably shouldn't drive any more today. I really need to relax."

And with this, I head back toward the front office to check out with Jesus.

(Saying a prayer for Armstrong along the way.)

He gives me a break on the $105 gate and only charges me $80. (Too dazed to count, I just walk.)

I thank Jesus, tip him 10 bucks and leave - wondering if I've hit a dead end... if I still have a job.

<u>**Acknowledgements**</u>

A super huge thanks to three very powerful witches
for making this book happen:
Mary Sack, Charity Sack and Edith McMullin.

Much additional thanks for help and guidance from:
Christian Lewis, Mike Nuell & Milo Sack.

Alex Sack is a taxi driver born in 1970 and raised in the Washington D.C. suburbs of Maryland. He attended several different colleges and universities around the D.C./Baltimore region as a music major for 4 & 1/2 years before quitting, pre-diploma, to the horror of his father. He tried his hand as a professional drummer and songwriter seeing him through travels domiciled in New York City's East Village, Los Angeles (where he scored a few songs on The Disney Channel's 'Even Stevens') and San Francisco - where he's ultimately put down roots. Alex is a single dad to two boys, currently ages 11 and (a full-fledged) 13. His post-natal fallback occupation as Operations Assistant at a start-up clean-tech engineering consultancy came to a sudden end with the one-two punch of the owner's fatal skiing accident in Tahoe and the subsequent downturn in the economy. This, and an acquired nervous twitch to cubicle work, has led to his latest job…

Made in the USA
San Bernardino, CA
11 January 2016